Decorating

MAGIC

Decorating Magic

500 Clever Tricks with 50 Easy-to-Find Items

Vanessa-Ann

Sterling Publishing Co., Inc. New York

A Sterling / Chapelle Book

Chapelle Ltd.:

Owner: Jo Packham

Editor: Laura Best

Photostylists: Jo Packham and Jill Dahlberg

Photography: Kevin Dilley for Hazen Imaging

Staff: Areta Bingham, Kass Burchett, Marilyn Goff,
Holly Hollingsworth, Susan Jorgensen,
Barbara Milburn, Linda Orton,
Karmen Quinney, Cindy Stoeckl
Kim Taylor, Sara Toliver, Desirée Wybrow

Library of Congress Cataloging-in-Publication Data

Vanessa-Ann Collection (Firm)
    Home dec magic : 500 clever tricks with 50 easy-to-find items
        / by Vanessa-Ann.
        p. cm.
    "A Sterling Chapelle book."
    Includes index.
    ISBN 0-8069-4133-2 Hardcover
          1-4027-0593-X Paperback
    1. Found objects (Art) in interior decoration. I. Title.

NK2115.5F68 V36 2002
747–dc21   2001049521

10 9 8 7 6 5 4 3 2 1

First paperback edition published in 2003 by
Sterling Publishing Company, Inc.
387 Park Avenue South, New York, NY 10016
©2002 by Vanessa-Ann
Distributed in Canada by Sterling Publishing
c/o Canadian Manda Group, One Atlantic Avenue, Suite 105
Toronto, Ontario, Canada M6K 3E7
Distributed in Great Britain by Chrysalis Books
64 Brewery Road, London N7 9NT England
Distributed in Australia by Capricorn Link (Australia) Pty. Ltd.
P.O. Box 704, Windsor, NSW 2756 Australia

Printed in China
All rights reserved

Sterling ISBN 0-8069-4133-2 Hardcover
            1-4027-0593-X Paperback

747
VAN
12-3-03-1

SPECIAL THANKS TO THE FOLLOWING DESIGNERS FOR THE FABULOUS IDEAS USED THROUGHOUT THIS BOOK:

DUTCH BELNAP, OGDEN, UT
ANITA LOUISE CRANE, PARK CITY, UT
JILL DAHLBERG, OGDEN, UT
DIANA DUNKLEY, PLEASANT VIEW, UT
LINDA DURBANO, LARAMIE, WY
KATHERYN ELLIOTT, WEST LINN, OR
JILL GROVER, BRIGHAM CITY, UT
MARY JO HINEY, LOS OSOS, CA
ROSSALYN MONTAGUE, OGDEN, UT

ALSO, A SPECIAL THANK YOU TO:

MIKE DILLON OF MUKILTEO, WA FOR SHARING THE PHOTOGRAPHS IN HIS BOOK, THE GREAT BIRDHOUSE BOOK, PUBLISHED THROUGH STERLING/CHAPELLE. VISIT HIS WEBSITE AT DILLONWORKS.COM

MARTHA YOUNG OF WHIMBLE DESIGNS FOR HER LACE DESIGN ON PAGE 22. WHIMBLE DESIGNS IS A WONDERFULLY WHIMSICAL GIFT STORE IN ATLANTA, GA. SEE ADDITIONAL DESIGNS IN MARTHA'S NEW BOOK, THE WORLD OF WHIMBLE WHIMSY, PUBLISHED THROUGH STERLING/CHAPELLE.

JODY LYONS OF JOLI JEWELRY IN BROOKLYN, NY FOR THE LAPEL PINS SHOWN ON PAGE 8. MORE OF JUDY'S BEAUTIFUL WORK CAN BE SEEN IN THE BOOK FLEA MARKET JEWELRY: NEW STYLE FROM OLD TREASURES, PUBLISHED THROUGH STERLING/CHAPELLE.

Vanessa-Ann

Vanessa-Ann consists of a number of talented artists and designers who design and create handcrafted pieces. The extraordinary stying of the photographs and the comprehensive finishing instructions are the company's unique signature and make their publications the most recognizable in the industry.

Since 1979 The Vanessa-Ann Collection also known by its parent company, Chapelle Limited, has authored and/or copub-

lished more than 150 hardbound titles on subjects ranging from decorating and gardening to master woodworking and antique needlework. Today, Vanessa-Ann and its top designers continue to provide an endless source of inspirational ideas to consumers requiring the most innovative designs and new product concepts.

With the help of the Vanessa-Ann staff, use your imagination to bring design and beauty into your home and garden. There is not just one right way to adorn your home—experiment with different colors, objects, and placement. There are a myriad of ways to bring a little change into your life and nothing is easier than to use an ordinary object in a new and unusual way. There is no right or wrong way. Explore and create. When your ideas come to life and you enjoy the results with every glance, you have succeeded in bringing imagination into your home in a manner others can enjoy.

The decorating and craft ideas in this book are suggestions only and are not considered complete. To learn more information on a particular technique, consult a professional or refer to books specifically addressing the desired topic.

Table of Contents

Buttons

1...TO MAKE A COLORFUL NECK-
LACE, STRING TWO SEED BEADS AND
A BRIGHT BUTTON ONTO THREAD.
REPEAT WITH NEW BUTTON AND
BEADS, BRINGING BUTTONS BACK-
TO-BACK, THEN CONTINUE.

2...USE VINTAGE BUTTONS TO MAKE
NEW LAPEL PINS AS JODY LYONS
DOES IN THIS PHOTOGRAPH.

3...PAINT SMALL DESIGNS ON
BLANK CARDS AND ATTACH
BUTTONS AND CHARMS.

4...CROCHET A BEAUTIFUL
NECKLACE WITH MOTHER-OF-
PEARL BUTTONS.

5...FILL A VINTAGE JAR WITH
ANTIQUE BUTTONS TO MAKE
AN UNUSUAL ACCENT PIECE.

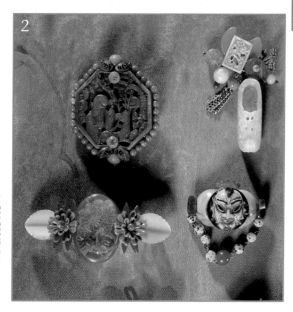

6...MAKE BUTTON TAGS TO ADD A PERSONAL TOUCH TO A GIFT.

7...GLUE VINTAGE BUTTONS TO A WOODEN PICTURE FRAME TO DISPLAY OLD FAMILY PHOTOGRAPHS.

8...ADD A BUTTON FACE TO FABRIC VEGETABLES OR FRUITS.

9...SEW BUTTONS AS CLOSURES FOR HANDMADE ENVELOPES.

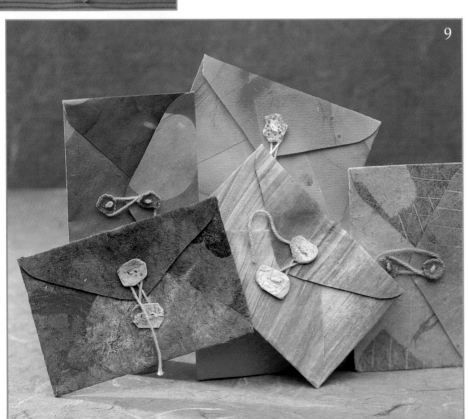

10...SEW TINY BUTTONS AND EMBROIDER FLOWER STEMS TO HOLD PHOTOGRAPHS ON SCRAPBOOK PAGES OR CARD FRONTS.

Notions

11...FOR A SEWING-ROOM PINCUSHION, TAKE AN ANTIQUE SPOOL, PAD WITH BATTING, COVER WITH FABRIC, AND ADORN WITH NOTIONS.

12...STRING BEADS AND PAINTED THREAD SPOOLS FOR A COLORFUL NECKLACE.

13...ADORN PLAIN WHITE CHILDREN'S KNEE SOCKS WITH BUTTONS AND PIECES OF LACE TO MAKE COLLECTIBLE CHRISTMAS ORNAMENTS.

14...USE A TOY WAGON FILLED WITH SPOOLS OF CROCHET THREAD FOR AN ACCENT PIECE.

15...DECORATE A PINECONE TREE WITH MINIATURE BEARS, THREAD SPOOLS, AND BASKETS.

16...DESIGN SMALL CHILDREN'S DRESS PINS BY GLUING PAINTED THIMBLES, BEADED LEAVES, AND SMALL BUTTON FLOWERS ONTO A PIN BACK.

17...USE WOODEN SPOOLS WRAPPED WITH THREAD AS DRAWER PULLS.

18...MAKE A SMALL SEWING BOX BY GLUING SPOOLS OF THREAD AROUND A CIRCULAR BASE AND ADDING A LID.

19...HANG BRIGHTLY COLORED TASSELS OVER A DOOR WINDOW TO ENSURE PRIVACY.

20...MAKE ADORABLE PARTY FAVORS WITH A FRESH LIME AND ODDS AND ENDS FROM THE SEWING BOX.

Tassels

24...USE A TASSEL FOR A CLO-SURE ON A DECORATIVE BOX.

25...A COLORED TASSEL MAKES AN ELEGANT BOOKMARK.

21...ADORN A GIFT WITH A HAND-TIED TASSEL.

22...ADDING A TASSEL TO A BED PILLOW ADDS TO THE DESIGN AND COLOR OF THE ROOM.

23...HANG TASSELS FROM DECORATIVE SHELVES.

26...ADD CHARM IN A GUEST BATHROOM BY SECURING A TASSEL AROUND TOWELS.

27...MAKE A DOOR EASIER TO PULL OPEN WITH A TASSEL.

28...BEAUTIFY A LAMP WITH A TASSEL LAMP PULL.

29...HANG TASSELS FROM SHOWER CURTAIN HOOKS FOR A "FAR EASTERN TOUCH."

30...USE A TASSEL TO EMBELLISH A PEN OR OTHER ART IMPLEMENT.

Scarves

31...CREATE A "DESIGNER STYLE" DOOR BETWEEN BEDROOMS BY HANGING A LONG SCARF.

32...WRAP A SILK SCARF AROUND A CHERISHED CERAMIC BUNNY.

33...USE AN EMBROIDERED SCARF TO TRIM A GUEST ROOM BED COVERING.

34...ATTACH SCARVES WITH DRAPERY CLIPS TO CREATE COLORFUL DRAPES. CLIPPING ALLOWS THE SCARVES TO BE EASILY REMOVED TO WEAR.

35...USE A DECORATIVE SCARF AS AN ELEGANT TABLECLOTH.

36...WRAP A GIFT WITH A SCARF.

38

37...TIE A SILK SCARF
AROUND A PLAIN,
INEXPENSIVE PILLOW.

38...SEW SIMPLE
SEAMS IN A LARGE
SCARF TO CREATE
A DECORATIVE COM-
PUTER COVER.

40

39

39...SWAG A LONG
LACE SCARF UNDER THE
MANTEL FOR AN ELE-
GANT CHRISTMAS CELE-
BRATION.

40...COVER A SELDOM
USED TELEVISION WITH
AN OVERSIZED FRINGED
SCARF.

Scarves

Quilts

41...USE SMALL PIECES FROM OLD QUILTS TO MAKE MINIA-TURE CHRISTMAS STOCKING ORNAMENTS.

42...ATTACH DRAPERY CLIPS AND HANG A SMALL QUILT IN PLACE OF A FRAMED PICTURE.

43...SEW A QUILT REMNANT INTO A SHABBY-CHIC TOASTER COVER.

44

45

44...USE VINTAGE QUILT
TOPS TO UPHOLSTER
ANTIQUE FURNITURE PIECES.

46

45...FASHION A QUILT INTO A
COUNTRY SHOWER CURTAIN.

46...STIFFEN AND SHAPE
A QUILT REMNANT INTO A
SMALL BASKET.

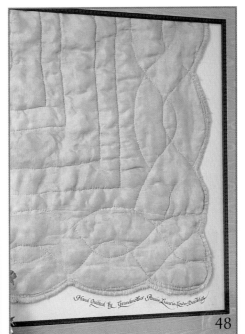

Hard Quilted by Grandmother Annie Laurie Leslie Dunfield

48

47...USE A VINTAGE BED QUILT AS A DRAP-ERY PANEL.

48...TAKE A SMALL SECTION FROM A MUCH-LOVED QUILT, FRAME IT, AND WRITE A FAVORITE APPLICABLE SAYING UNDERNEATH.

49...CUT AND SEW A VINTAGE QUILT INTO A NEW BABY BASINETTE AND PILLOWS.

50...USE A SECTION FROM A WORN-OUT QUILT TO MAKE A THROW PILLOW.

49

50

Hats

53...DRESS UP A BED BY USING HATS IN PLACE OF DECORATIVE PILLOWS.

54...ADD COLOR TO A PATIO BY HANGING COLORFUL HATS NEXT TO HAND-PAINTED, FLOWER-FILLED RAINGUTTERS.

55...TO DRESS UP A PLAIN STRAW HAT, WATERCOLOR YOUR FAVORITE DESIGN, AND ADD A VINTAGE CROCHETED FLOWER.

51...CREATE A HAT STAND FROM TWIGS TIED TOGETHER AND DECORATED WITH BERRIES. USE TO DISPLAY A HAT FOR A DECORATIVE ACCENT IN PLACE OF A VASE OF FLOWERS.

52...GIVE AN OLD STRAW HAT AS A SPECIAL GIFT "BOX" TO HOLD GARDEN SEEDS AND MINIATURE GARDENING ITEMS FOR YOUR FAVORITE GARDENER.

56...PLACE A DECORATED VINTAGE HAT ON THE NIGHTSTAND TO COVER A BOX FILLED WITH VALUABLES.

57...DECORATE A BALL CAP FOR A FESTIVE OCCASION WITH RIBBONS, BUTTONS, AND CHARMS.

58...USE CHILDREN'S HATS AS PINCUSHIONS. STUFF INSIDE OF HAT WITH BATTING AND COVER THE BOTTOM WITH A PIECE OF FELT.

59...BRING CHARACTER TO A ROOM WITH AN OLD HAT, GLOVES, AND GARDEN SUPPLIES.

60...HANG AN ANTIQUE HAT RACK TO DISPLAY FAVORITE HATS AND SCARVES.

Lace

64...DRESS UP A BEDROOM TABLE BY ADDING PIECES OF TATTED LACE TO A DECORATIVE BOX.

65...COVER A JOURNAL WITH SCRAPS OF OLD LACE.

61...LIGHTLY TACK A VINTAGE FILET CROCHET TABLE RUNNER TO THE EDGE OF A FIREPLACE MANTEL.

62...FRAME A PIECE OF YOUR GRANDMOTHER'S OLD LACE BETWEEN TWO PIECES OF GLASS IN AN INTERIOR WINDOW AS MARTHA YOUNG OF WHIMBLE DESIGNS DID.

63...FOLD BATTENBERG LACE AROUND MINTS FOR WONDERFUL GUEST FAVORS.

66...USE A COLLECTION OF LACE SQUARES TO PIECE TOGETHER A QUILT TOP.

67...ADD ELEGANCE TO A BEDROOM BY COVERING A FLOWER VASE WITH A LACE CLOTH.

68...SEW LAYERS OF EYELET LACE-EDGED FABRIC INTO A FLOUNCY TREE SKIRT.

69...DECORATE DRESS SHOES WITH LACE AND BEADS.

70...SEW COLORFUL LACE TO A LITTLE GIRL'S FAVORITE SOCKS.

Doilies

71... DECOUPAGE PIECES OF OLD DOILIES AROUND THE EDGE OF A WOODEN FRAME.

72...SOFTEN A SERVING TRAY WITH A DOILY LINER.

73...SEW DOILIES INTO A COUNTRY QUILT.

74...TURN A SMALL STOOL INTO A HANDY DISPLAY TABLE WITH THE ADDITION OF A DOILY TOPPER.

75... DRAPE A LARGE DOILY OVER A LAMP SHADE TO CREATE SOFT, BEAUTIFUL LIGHT.

76... TIE POTPOURRI TO THE CENTER OF A DOILY FOR A SWEET-SMELLING SACHET.

77...FOR A GUEST BED AND BATH, WRAP TOWELS IN HEIRLOOM DOILIES.

78... ADD ELEGANCE TO A GIFT BY ADDING A DOILY TO THE WRAP.

79... CREATE A LOVELY PHOTOGRAPH MAT WITH PAPER LACE DOILIES.

80... ADD A BIT OF ELEGANCE BY ADHERING A PAPER DOILY TO A CHRISTMAS TREE STAR.

Ribbons

81...PLACE A PHOTOGRAPH BETWEEN TWO PIECES OF GLASS, TIE, AND HANG WITH RIBBON.

82...WRAP WIDE RIBBON AROUND A FABRIC SACHET BAG TO MAKE A FANCY GIFT.

83...ENHANCE A PLAIN THROW PILLOW WITH A LARGE RIBBON BOW.

84...HANG RIBBON SPOOLS ON CURTAIN RODS AND ATTACH INSIDE A CUPBOARD TO BEAUTIFULLY ORGANIZE YOUR NOTIONS.

85...HANG EVERYDAY SCISSORS FROM A PIECE OF RIBBON TO STAY ORGANIZED IN A PRETTY WAY.

86...HANG RIBBONS FROM A SHORT CUR-
TAIN ROD AND USE AS A WALL ACCENT.

87...WRAP WIDE ORGANZA RIBBON
AROUND A SMALL LAMP SHADE TO CHANGE
WITH THE MOOD OR THE SEASONS.

88...FILL A DECORATIVE BOTTLE WITH BUB-
BLE BATH, TOP WITH A WINE CORK, AND TIE
A SILK RIBBON AND BEADED TASSEL FOR A
BEAUTIFUL GIFT.

89...WRAP A LAMP
SHADE WITH WIDE
RIBBON.

90...WRAP AND TIE
LONG SILK RIBBONS
AROUND A PLAIN
GLASS VASE FOR A
MORE SOPHISTICAT-
ED APPEAL.

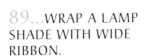

Bed & Bath Linens

91...CONVERT A VINTAGE LINEN BED SCARF INTO A SMALL POCKET FOR THE INSIDE OF A BASKET OR BAG.

92...SEW WASH CLOTHS INTO PLAYTIME MONSTERS.

93...USE A SHEET AS A BOHEMIAN-STYLE CHAIR COVER.

94...DRAPE HAND TOWELS OVER A TENSION ROD AND TIE ON TINY STUFFED ANI-MALS FOR A NEW-BORN BABY'S CURTAINS.

95...SCENT BED LINENS WITH LAVENDER WATER DURING IRONING AND TUCK SPRIGS OF LAVENDER IN PILLOWCASE FOR SLEEPING.

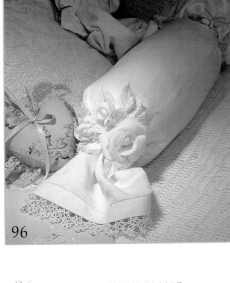

96...ROLL A LINEN HAND TOWEL AROUND A NECK-ROLL PILLOW, THEN TIE ENDS WITH RIBBONS AND SILK FLOWERS.

97...THROW BEDSPREADS AND BLANKETS OVER LIVING-ROOM FURNITURE FOR A CONTEMPORARY DECORATOR APPROACH TO SLIPCOVERS.

98...DRESS UP A PATIO TABLE AND CHAIRS BY DRAPING AND TYING A SHEET OVER THE TABLE. THEN TEAR OLD SHEETS INTO THIN STRIPS AND WRAP METAL CHAIR BACKS AND LEGS. FINALLY, COVER THE CHAIR SEATS WITH THE SAME FABRIC FOR AN EASY DECORATOR TOUCH.

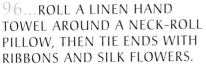

99...STORE EXTRA PILLOWCASES AND LINENS IN A SHELL-COVERED POT ON THE NIGHTSTAND.

100...HANG SMALL VINTAGE HAND TOWELS FOR A CAFÉ CURTAIN ACROSS A WINDOW.

Worn
Wearables

101...APPLIQUÉ A FLANNEL SHIRT ONTO A PURCHASED BED QUILT.

102...PLACE A VINTAGE BALL GOWN ON AN ANTIQUE DRESS FORM; DECORATE WITH LIGHTS AND ORNAMENTS TO USE AS A "CHRISTMAS TREE."

103...USE DENIM CUTOFFS AS A DRAPERY VALANCE IN A YOUNG COWPOKE'S BEDROOM.

104...DISPLAY CHERISHED CLOTHING SUCH AS BLESSING, BAPTISMAL, AND CONFIRMATION DRESSES.

105...A VINTAGE DRESS HANGING IN THE KITCHEN ADDS TO THE FUN COUNTRY STYLE.

106...HANG A JAPANESE KIMONO AS AN ETHNIC WALL DECORATION.

107

109

107...HANG A CHERISHED PIECE OF BABY'S CLOTHING ON AN EXPANDABLE ROD TO KEEP MEMORIES ALIVE.

108...DRESS COLLECTIBLE TEDDY BEARS IN CHILDREN'S ANTIQUE CLOTHING.

108

110

109...APPLIQUÉ VINTAGE BABY CLOTHING TO THE FRONT OF A QUILT THAT WILL HANG IN A GRAND-DAUGHTER'S ROOM.

110...FOR A GUEST BEDROOM, FRAME LACY LADIES' HANKIES AS SHABBY-CHIC STYLE WALL DÉCOR.

Worn Wearables

Shoes

111

112

111...CONVERT A BABY BOOTIE INTO A CHER-
ISHED PINCUSHION.

112...EMBELLISH CHILDREN'S OUTGROWN
BALLET SLIPPERS AND USE THEM AS PART OF
THEIR ROOM DÉCOR.

113...USING VINTAGE EARRINGS GLUED TO
PUSH PINS, HANG ANTIQUE VELVET SLIPPERS
ON THE WALL.

114...SECURE THE TOE OF A HIGH-HEEL SHOE
TO THE INSOLE, THEN HANG THE SHOE FOR A
VERY "KAMPY" JEWELRY HOOK.

115...ADD COLOR TO THE GARDEN BY CON-
VERTING A PAIR OF CHILDREN'S GALOSHES
INTO A WEATHERPROOF FLOWER PLANTER.

Purses & Suitcases

116...HANG A BEADED EVENING BAG IN A WALL GROUPING TO BE ADMIRED UNTIL IT IS USED.

117...ADD A COLLECTIBLE VINTAGE PURSE TO AN ACCENT GROUPING ON A BOOKSHELF OR COFFEE TABLE.

118...MAKE YOUR FAVORITE RETRO CROCHETED DOILIES INTO A SMALL EVENING BAG.

119...HANG A TEENAGER'S "ONCE FAVORITE, NOW DISCARDED" PURSE IN HER ROOM WITH HER FAVORITE TINY TEDDY BEAR.

120...DISPLAY A BELOVED BEAR IN AN OLD SUITCASE IN THE LIVING ROOM.

121

122

124

121...HANG A '50S CROCHETED PURSE IN THE BATH AREA AS A WASHCLOTH HOLDER.

122...FAUX-FINISH AN OLD SUITCASE TO USE AS ADDITIONAL STORAGE IN A CHILD'S ROOM.

123...STACK SUITCASES TO CREATE AN END TABLE IN THE BEDROOM. THESE WILL ALSO PROVIDE ADDITIONAL STORAGE SPACE.

124...DISPLAY BELOVED TREASURES IN A WICKER SUITCASE IN THE CORNER OF A DEN.

125...ADD LEGS TO THE BOTTOM OF AN OLD TRUNK FOR A FASHIONABLE COFFEE TABLE.

123

125

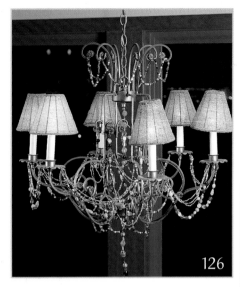

126

Jewelry

127

128

126...DRAPE BEADS OVER A CHANDELIER TO ADD DESIGN, LIGHT, AND COLOR.

127...ADD A STRING OF PEARLS TO AN OIL LAMP FOR A TOUCH OF ELEGANCE.

128...STRING INEXPENSIVE NECKLACES TOGETHER FOR A BEADED DIVIDER.

129...WEIGHT CLOTH NAPKIN CORNERS WITH OLD JEWELRY AND CHARMS TO KEEP FOOD COVERED.

130...ADD AN ADDITIONAL TOUCH OF ELEGANCE TO ANY VASE BY SIMPLY DRAPING STRANDS OF PEARLS.

129

130

131...MAKE ECLECTIC NAPKIN RINGS WITH BRACELETS, VINTAGE PINS, AND EARRINGS—NOTHING NEEDS TO MATCH.

132...GLUE MAGNETS TO THE BACK OF ECLECTIC JEWELRY PIECES.

133...ATTACH DIME-STORE EARRINGS TO THE EDGE OF A LONG SCARF AND USE AS A TABLE RUNNER.

134...GLUE PIECES FROM OLD EARRINGS TO THE EDGE OF VOTIVE HOLDERS.

135...DECORATE A GIFT BOX BY ADDING BROKEN AND DISCARDED JEWELRY PIECES TO THE RIBBONS.

Umbrellas

136...ADD BRIGHTLY COLORED TASSELS AND FRINGE FOR A BOHEMIAN-STYLE PATIO UMBRELLA.

137...COLOR A DARKENED CORNER WITH A COLLECTIBLE FLORAL-PATTERNED UMBRELLA.

138...COVER A FIREPLACE OPENING IN THE SUMMER WITH AN UMBRELLA.

139...BRING ATTENTION AND SHADE TO A LEMONADE STAND WITH COLORFUL UMBRELLAS.

140...SECURE AN UMBRELLA OVER A CHILD'S BED FOR A FUN CANOPY.

141...SUSPEND UMBRELLAS FROM THE CEILING FOR AN ORIENTAL FLARE.

142...HANG ADDITIONAL PATIO LIGHTING FROM A PATIO UMBRELLA TO ADD INTEREST.

143...DRAPE BATTENBERG LACE TABLE RUNNERS OVER A PATIO UMBRELLA FOR A SPECIAL OCCASION.

144...ENHANCE A BATHROOM WINDOW TREATMENT WITH AN ORIENTAL UMBRELLA.

145...SHADE AND DECORATE AN OUTDOOR GAZEBO WITH A NUMBER OF MATCHING UMBRELLAS.

146

Apothecary & Mason Jars

147

148

149

146...FOR SOAKING IN THE BATH, FILL OLD APOTHECARY JARS WITH BATH SALTS AND SCENTS.

147...STORE AND DISPLAY COLORFUL THREAD OR BUTTONS IN A MASON JAR.

148...WRAP AN APOTHECARY JAR WITH A HAND-PRINTED LABEL AND USE AS A VASE FOR SILK AND PAPER FLOWERS.

149...PAINT A MASON JAR, FILL WITH SAND, AND ADD A VOTIVE CANDLE. JARS CAN ALSO BE PLACED OUTSIDE AS LUMINARIES.

150... USE A MASON JAR WITH AN ORNAMENT FOR A LID TO "WRAP" A CHRISTMAS CANDY GIFT.

151... ACCENTUATE THE TABLE WITH A MASON JAR FILLED WITH BREADSTICKS.

152... DRESS UP CANNED FRUIT OR VEG-ETABLES WITH LACE DOILIES AND "LABEL" WITH FABRIC STRIPS.

153... GIVE YOUR FAVORITE BUG COL-LECTOR A "BUG" DESIGNED T-SHIRT IN A BUG-CATCHING JAR.

154... USE YOUR CANNED FRUITS AND VEGETABLES AS WALL ART IN YOUR KITCHEN.

155... CREATE A BEAUTIFUL ARRANGEMENT USING GLASS SHELVING TO DISPLAY COLORED APOTHECARY JARS.

Terra-cotta Pots

158...STUFF A PAINTED POT WITH BATTING. ADD A FABRIC TOP AND RIBBON TRIM TO MAKE A CUSTOM-TAILORED PINCUSHION FOR ANY ROOM IN THE HOUSE.

159...PAINT AND GLUE GRADUATING-SIZED POTS TOGETHER TO CREATE A COLORFUL "FLOWER DOLL" FOR THE GARDEN.

156...PAINT MINIATURE POTS WITH COORDINAT-ING COLORS, DRILL A HOLE IN THE BOTTOM, AND USE FOR NAPKIN RINGS. ADD THESE TO NAPKINS IN A LARGE PAINTED POT AND USE FOR TABLETOP DESIGNER STORAGE.

157...DECOUPAGE WRAPPING TISSUE AROUND A POT AND FILL WITH MINIATURE GIFTS TO DISPLAY OR GIVE AWAY.

160...MAKE A PLACE CARD WITH MINIATURE SILK FLOWERS IN A POT AND PLACE ON A MINIATURE CHAIR.

161...TURN A SEASHELL-MOSAIC POT UPSIDE DOWN IN A FOUNTAIN FOR ADDITIONAL DECORATION.

162...MINGLE BROKEN POTS AND COLORFUL PLANTS TO CREATE AN UNUSUAL GARDEN CORNER.

163

164

165

163...A PAINTED POT CAN BECOME A DELIGHTFUL WIND CHIME BY HANGING MINIATURE GARDEN TOOLS THROUGH THE DRAINAGE HOLE.

164...STACK FLORAL-PAINTED POTS AND PLUMB THE GROUPING FOR AN OUTDOOR FOUNTAIN.

165...CREATE A UNIQUE GIFT WRAPPING BY PLACING GOODIES IN POTS AND TYING A BOW OVER THE INVERTED SAUCER.

166

167

168

Bottles & Vases

169

166...FILL INEXPENSIVE PLAIN BOT-TLES, VASES, AND BOWLS WITH SAND, SHELLS, AND CANDLES; THEN TOP WITH OLD GLASS LAMP SHADES.

167...FILL A DECORATIVE BOTTLE WITH HONEY AND CINNAMON. SEAL, THEN TIE ON A HONEY DIPPER FOR A SWEET GIFT.

168...USE MORE THAN ONE VASE AS A CENTERPIECE. REPEAT THE VASES AND THEIR CONTENTS TO ADD CHARM TO A PLAIN INEXPEN-SIVE TABLE DECORATION.

169...STORE VINEGAR, OILS, AND OTHER EDIBLES IN GLASS BOTTLES "CORKED" WITH MARBLES, OLD GLASS CHANDELIER PARTS, OR GLASS TOPPERS.

170

171

170...USE A LARGE METAL VASE AS A STYLISH ICE BUCKET.

171...USE EMPTY JUICE BOTTLES IN THE BATHROOM TO HOLD NECESSARY BATH ITEMS.

172...WRITE A NOTE AND USE A VINTAGE BOTTLE AS THE "ENVELOPE."

172

174

175

173...MAKE PANTRY SELECTIONS EASIER AND BEAUTIFY YOUR OPEN SHELVES WITH VARIOUS BOTTLES HOLDING YOUR PERISHABLES.

174...SERVE WINE IN A HAND-PAINTED BOTTLE.

175...DECOUPAGE CUT-OUT LEAVES ONTO A WINE BOTTLE FOR A RETRO CANDLEHOLDER.

Glassware

176...INVERT A BRANDY SNIFTER, PILSNER BEER GLASS, OR COCKTAIL GLASS TO FRAME A FAVORITE PICTURE.

177...USE MARGARITA GLASSES TO HOLD PARTY DIPS AND SAUCES.

178...CREATE A COLORFUL SHELF WITH INVERTED GOBLETS.

179...MAKE AN EASY FRUIT TRAY WITH STACKED GLASS BOWLS, CUPS, AND SAUCERS.

180

182

181

180...ADAPT A COFFEE CUP INTO A
SHAVING MUG.

181...TURN ICE CREAM GLASSES INTO
CANDLEHOLDERS FOR A SUMMER
GARDEN PARTY.

182...USE A CUT-CRYSTAL WINE
GLASS AS A VASE FOR FRESHLY PICKED
GARDEN ROSES.

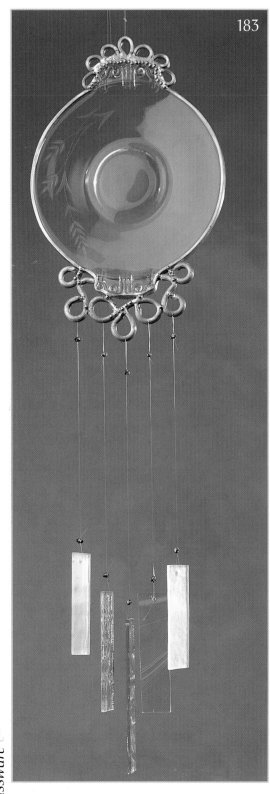

183

183...CONVERT A DECORATIVE GLASS SAUCER INTO A STYLISH WIND CHIME.

184...INVERT GLASSES AND GOBLETS ON GLASS SAUCERS TO MAKE A DELIGHTFUL CANDY DISH.

185...PAINT WINE GLASSES WITH FLOWERS, SECURE IN FLOWERPOTS PAINTED TO MATCH, AND PLACE CANDLES IN THE GLASSES.

184

185

187

Kitchenware

188

186...DISPLAY
LOVELY GARDEN
FLOWERS IN COF-
FEE MUGS AND
FLOUR SIFTERS.

187...CONVERT A
PEWTER DRINKING
GLASS INTO A
CANDLEHOLDER.

188...USE A VIN-
TAGE KITCHEN
CRATE TO HOLD
OLD MILK BOT-
TLES FOR FLOWER
ARRANGEMENTS
ALL THROUGH
THE YEAR.

189...PAINT AND DRESS WOODEN SPOONS AND SPATULAS TO SCARE EVEN THE BRAVEST HALLOWEEN DINNER GUESTS.

190...USE AN OLD STOVE AS A UNIQUE OUTDOOR PLANTER.

191...BRIGHTEN THE KITCHEN WITH A UNIQUE OIL LAMP MADE BY FILLING A BLENDER WITH ARTIFICIAL STRAWBERRIES AND LAMP OIL.

192

193

194

192...DISPLAY AN OLD TEA SET ON THE MANTEL AS CHIC PLANTERS.

193...SHOW OFF FAMILY PHOTO-GRAPHS, USING A KITCHEN FUNNEL AS AN UNUSUAL PICTURE HOLDER.

194...SERVE STEAMING ARTICHOKES INSIDE SHINY NEW STEAMERS—THEY ARE FUNKY ON METAL PLATES.

195...PAINT CLAY POTS FOREST GREEN, FILL WITH MINIATURE PINECONES, AND INSERT COOKIE CUTTERS ON A STICK. USE AS A HOLIDAY KITCHEN DECORATION.

195

Silverware

196...WRITE ON THE FLAT HANDLE OF A PIECE OF SILVER WITH A PERMANENT MARKER WHEN USING AS A GIFT TAG.

197...ATTACH MAGNETS TO SILVERWARE AND USE TO HOLD PHOTOGRAPHS IN THE KITCHEN.

198...OLD SILVERWARE MAKES SWEET MUSIC IN A MOSAIC WIND CHIME.

199...WIRE SEVERAL SPOONS TOGETHER FOR A KITCHEN CANDLEHOLDER.

200...WIRE DISCARDED SERVING SPOONS AND FORKS TO AN OLD FENCE, CREATING A FUNKY PLANT DISPLAY.

201...FRAME GRANDMOTHER'S SILVER WITH OLD LETTERS OR POSTCARDS TO MAKE MEMORABLE PIECES OF ART FOR THE WALL.

202...PLACE EVERYDAY SILVER IN A CLEAR DECANTER AND KEEP IT ON THE TABLE OR COUNTER, FREEING UP DRAWER SPACE.

203...BEND FORK PRONGS TO FORM A SMALL VINTAGE SILVER HOLDER FOR FAVORITE PICTURES.

204...CUT OFF THE END OF A PIECE OF SILVER, DRILL A HOLE, AND CREATE A KEY CHAIN.

205...A MISMATCHED FORK IN A JAR OF HERBS OR SPICES MAKES NOT ONLY A HANDY RECIPE HOLDER BUT ALSO A JAR OF POTPOURRI.

Tins & Pans

208...A MUFFIN TIN MAKES A GREAT VOTIVE CANDLEHOLDER FOR THE KITCHEN OR GARDEN.

209...USE A NEW BAKING TIN AS A SERVING TRAY FOR OUTDOOR BARBEQUES.

206...COPPER PANS MAKE WONDERFUL DESIGN TOUCHES IN A KITCHEN OR DINING ROOM.

207...USE A VARIETY OF RUSTIC KITCHEN PANS TO HOLD POTPOURRI.

211

210...USE AN OLD LOAF PAN TO STORE RECIPE CARDS.

210

212

211...USE MUFFIN TINS AS CONTAINERS FOR STARTING SEEDS. THEY WILL LOOK GREAT IN YOUR KITCHEN WINDOW.

212...A FONDUE PAN MAKES A STURDY PLANTER WHILE FONDUE FORKS ARE COLORFUL PLANT STAKES.

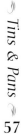

213...LIVEN UP YOUR DAUGHTER'S BATHROOM WITH BRIGHT COLORS. USE A STURDY COOKIE SHEET AS THE BACKGROUND FOR FUNKY SLIPPER ARTWORK. A MUFFIN TIN KEEPS HAIR ACCESSORIES ORGANIZED.

214...HANG LARGE OLD POTS AND PANS ON THE OUTSIDE OF A COUNTRY HOME TO BRING AN ADDED BIT OF NOSTALGIA TO THE GROWING HOLLYHOCKS.

214

213

215

215...BRING PARTY DECORATIONS AS A BIRTHDAY GIFT, DIVIDED ARTISTICALLY IN THE CUPS OF A MUFFIN TIN.

Kitchen Linens

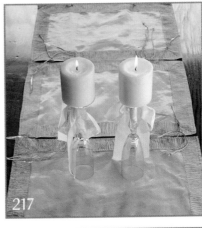

216

217

218

219

216...DECORATE PLAIN BATH TOWELS WITH LINEN NAPKINS.

217...CREATE A NEW TABLE RUNNER BY CONNECTING SEVERAL PLACE MATS TOGETHER WITH GROMMETS, THEN TIE WITH RIBBONS.

218...USE WOVEN TWIG PLACE MATS AS DRAPERY VALANCES ON FRENCH DOORS.

219...SEW TWO PLACE MATS TOGETHER ON THREE SIDES. STITCH IN THREE POCKET DIVIDERS AND USE FOR INDIVIDUAL PICNIC PLACE MATS THAT EASILY STORE NAPKINS AND SILVERWARE.

220...USE LACE TABLE RUNNERS TO DRAPE OVER SHOWER DOORS FOR SHOWER CURTAINS.

221...GROMMET TWO NAPKINS ON EACH OF FOUR SIDES, PLACE OVER PLAIN THROW PILLOW, AND TIE WITH RIBBONS.

222...CLIP FOLDED TABLE RUNNERS ON A GARDEN POTTING BENCH TO HIDE TOOLS AND EMPTY POTS.

224...DRAPE A LACE TABLECLOTH OVER A LIVING-ROOM CHAIR FOR A TOUCH OF ELEGANCE.

225...TAKE A SMALL SQUARE TABLECLOTH, DECOUPAGE TO PAINTER'S CANVAS, COVER WITH SHELLAC, TRIM EDGES WITH FABRIC BAND AND TASSELS, AND USE AS A FLOOR CLOTH.

223...TAKE FLOUR-SACK DISHTOWELS, EMBROIDER A SAYING ON EACH, AND SEW INTO SMALL CHRISTMAS STOCKING ORNAMENTS.

Buckets

226

227

228

229

226...ADORN THE PORCH WITH A BUCKET FULL OF SHELLS AND PLANTS.

227...USE A SMALL BUCKET IN THE BED-ROOM TO HOLD COL-LECTIBLES.

228...FILL A GARDEN BUCKET WITH ICE FOR COOLING BEVERAGES.

229...CARRY LUNCH TO THE BEACH IN A DECO-RATED SAND PAIL.

230...HOLD PENS AND PENCILS IN SMALL BUCKETS IN THE KITCHEN OR OFFICE.

230

231

232

231...DISPLAY A REFLECTIVE GARDEN BALL IN A BUCKET OF PRODUCE AND FLOWERS FROM THE GARDEN.

232...FLOAT TEA LIGHTS IN A BUCKET FOR LIGHT AT A GARDEN PARTY.

233...DRIP PAINT DOWN THE SIDES OF NEW UNUSED PAINT BUCKETS TO USE AS "GIFT BOXES."

234

233

235

234...ADORN A WALL WITH A SELECTION OF COLORFUL SAP BUCKETS.

235...FILL METAL BUCKETS WITH FRESH FLOWERS AND ARRANGE ON THE BATH-ROOM VANITY FOR A FRESH LOOK ALL DAY.

236

237

Cans

238

239

236...DECORATE CLEANED SOUP CANS TO BE USED AS GIFT CONTAINERS.

237...TAKE VINTAGE SOUP OR OTHER KITCHEN CANS, ADD SMALL TEDDY BEARS AND OTHER MINIATURES TO DECORATE KITCHEN SHELVES.

238...PLACE SERVING TRAY ON INVERTED CANS TO ADD A UNIQUE CENTERPIECE.

239...CANS OF ALL SHAPES AND SIZES MAKE PERFECT FLOATING-CANDLE CONTAINERS FOR THE GARDEN.

240...FILL AN OLD WEATHERED CAN WITH FRESH GARDEN FLOWERS.

241

241...COVER LIDDED CANS WITH PAPER, EMBELLISH WITH LACE, RIBBON, AND SILK FLOW-ERS AND USE AS STORAGE CONTAINERS.

242...CONVERT A CLEANED SOUP CAN INTO A GIRL'S JEWELRY BOX.

243...FILL A SOUP CAN WITH JELLY BEANS FOR DECORATING OR GIFT GIVING.

242

244

243

245

244...DECORATE UNOPENED FOOD CANS WITH MINIA-TURES TO USE AS BOOKENDS FOR COOKBOOKS.

245...RECYCLE EMPTY FILM CANS BY USING THEM TO WRAP SMALL GIFTS SUCH AS JEWELRY.

246...DECORATE A PLAIN PAPER BAG WITH A HANDLE FOR INEXPENSIVE GIFTWRAPPING.

247...MAKE HOLIDAY DECO-RATIONS BY PAINTING AND EMBELLISHING PLAIN BROWN PAPER BAGS.

Paper
Bags

248...WHITE OR NATURAL PAPER BAGS MAKE RECYCLABLE AND INEX-PENSIVE WRAPPING PAPER.

249...HANG DECORATED PAPER GIFT BAGS IN A CHILD'S ROOM TO ORGANIZE COLORED PENCILS AND CRAYONS, PUZZLE PIECES, HAIR ACCESSORIES, ETC.

250...TEAR PAPER BAGS INTO A VARIETY OF SIZES, DECOUPAGE ON FLOORS OR WALLS.

251

252

253

251...DESIGN ANIMAL GIFT BAGS FOR CHILDREN'S GIFTS WITH COLORED PAPER AND PENS.

252...USING LARGE PAPER BAGS, CUT OUT COWBOY BOOT BORDER TO LINE SHELVES. OUTLINE BOOTS WITH POPCORN CRUMBS AND ORANGE PEELS CUT INTO DESIGNS.

253...FASHION BEAUTIFUL CALENDAR PAGES OUT OF NEW PAPER BAGS CUT TO ACCOMMODATE DATES AND SEASONAL CROSS-STITCHED PROJECTS.

254...MAKE "ART BAGS" TO USE FOR STORAGE OF DELICATE ITEMS OR TO "WRAP" SPECIAL GIFTS BY DECOUPAGING SELECTED IMAGES AND ADDING RIBBONS AND PIECES OF JEWELRY.

255...STORE FRESH FRUITS AND VEGETABLES IN PAPER BAGS ON COUNTERTOP TO ALLOW THEM TO RIPEN NATURALLY.

254

255

Baskets

257

256...FILL A TIGHTLY WOVEN BASKET, TRIMMED TO LOOK LIKE A SNOWMAN, WITH POPCORN AND USE THE HAT AS A LID.

257...PREVENT LOSING THE REMOTE CONTROL BY KEEPING IT IN A SMALL BASKET IN THE FAMILY ROOM.

258...USE A COLLECTION OF BASKETS TO HOLD GARDEN PRODUCE.

259...A LARGE BASKET MAKES A GREAT BREAD COVER FOR A PATIO GATHERING.

260...PERSONAL NECESSITIES ARE "PRETTIER" IN BATHROOM CUPBOARDS WHEN PUT IN BRIGHTLY COLORED BASKETS.

258

259

260

264...USE A PICNIC BASKET AS ADDITIONAL STORAGE FOR LINEN.

265...WRAP FATHER'S DAY GIFTS IN A "DRESSED-UP" BASKET.

261...USE ROUND FLAT BASKETS AS AN ACCENT TO SWAGGED DRAPES.

262...SERVE BREAKFAST IN BED ON A VINTAGE WOVEN BASKET TRAY.

263...OFFER PARTY NUTS AND CANDIES IN A SELECTION OF SMALL BASKETS.

266

267

Toys

270

266...SURROUND A CHILD'S WADING POOL WITH HAND-PAINTED FENCE STAKES, FILL WITH DIRT, AND USE AS A CONTAINED GARDEN.

267...MAKE "ENTERTAINING" PLACE MATS BY OFFERING BLACKBOARDS AND CHALK.

268...PUT GUMBALL MACHINE PRIZES TO USE BY CREATING A COLORFUL MOSAIC ROOF FOR A BIRDHOUSE.

268

269

269...LEGOS® CAN BE CREATIVE BUILDING BLOCKS FOR ADULTS, MAKING SUCH MASTERPIECES AS A HOUSE TO HOLD THE WORKINGS OF A MUSIC BOX.

270...A CHILD'S PLASTIC BEACH BUCKET IS THE PERFECT CONTAINER TO HOLD MUFFIN MIX, MIXING "SHOVEL," AND RECIPE.

271...ATTACH A LIFELIKE PLASTIC FROG TO A KITCHEN CUPBOARD FOR A HANDLE.

272...USE A MARBLE CHESSBOARD AS A FINE SERVING TRAY.

273...SECURE PUZZLE PIECES AROUND A PICTURE FRAME TO GIVE CHILDLIKE CHARM.

274...FILL A CHILD'S ANTIQUE TRUCK WITH HOLIDAY TREATS FOR A FUN SERVING TRAY.

275...CREATE A CHRISTMAS DECORATION HOLDER FOR THE MANTEL, USING AN OLD TOY LOG CABIN.

276

Eggs

278

277

276...SHARE A SPRINGTIME GIFT ADORNED WITH A TINY WIRE NEST FULL OF RIBBON EGGS.

277...USE A COUNTRY-PAINTED EGG AS A STOPPER FOR FRESH MILK.

278...A BROKEN CERAMIC EGG TEMPORARILY GLUED BACK TOGETHER IS THE PERFECT WRAPPING FOR A SENTIMENTAL GIFT.

280

279

279...HIDE A SURPRISE ANNOUNCEMENT INSIDE A PERSONALIZED EGG.

280...DISPLAY PAINTED CERAMIC EGGS IN PAPER EGG CARTONS FOR A NATURAL TOUCH OF COUNTRY.

281...GENTLY CRACK EGG TOPS, EMPTY, AND WASH. STACK EGGS, GLUE TOGETHER, AND FILL WITH BEAD WAX. ADD WICK TO MAKE A DELICATE SPRING CANDLE.

282...DECORATE AN "EASTER TREE" BY WRAPPING PAINTED WOODEN EGGS WITH NETTING, TYING WITH RIBBONS, AND HANGING FROM A SMALL INDOOR TREE.

283...DYE EASTER EGGS SOLID COLORS, THEN WRAP WITH VARIEGATED FLOSS AND TINY CHARMS.

284...PAINT WOODEN EGGS IN COLORFUL PATTERNS TO DISPLAY.

285...CELEBRATE A BIRTH-DAY WITH "EGG CONES" FILLED WITH TREATS.

Eggs

Pumpkins & Gourds

286

287

288

286...FILL A HOLLOWED-OUT PUMPKIN WITH DRIED FLOWERS AND LEAVES.

287...COVER A PUMPKIN WITH TWO SHORT TABLE RUNNERS AND SECURE WITH WIRE. ADD GARLAND, A TWIG FOR THE STEM, AND A BOW.

288...CUT A HOLE IN THE TOP OF MINIA-TURE PUMPKINS AND STEADY A CANDLE IN THE CENTER OF EACH PUMPKIN.

289...CREATE A PUMPKIN LANTERN WITH ELECTRIC LIGHTS, GARNISHED WITH PEP-PERCORN, CRANBERRIES, AND GREENS.

290...SPRAY PUMPKINS GOLD FOR A TOUCH OF ELEGANCE.

289

290

291

293

295

291...CARVE AND PAINT A GOURD TO MAKE A TRULY UNIQUE PIECE OF ART.

292...WRAP WIRE AROUND A PUMPKIN STEM, THEN CURL LIKE GRAPEVINES. ADD A FEW LEAF SHAPES CUT FROM OLD SCREENS FOR AN UNUSUAL CENTERPIECE.

294

293...CUT OFF GOURD TOP, DECORATE AND FILL WITH BIRD SEED, THEN PLACE IN GARDEN.

294...INSERT MINIATURE PUMPKINS INTO A FLORAL ARRANGEMENT FOR ADDED TEXTURE.

295...ADD MINIATURE PUMPKINS TO AN AUTUMN CENTERPIECE TO BRING THE SEASON TO THE TABLE.

296

297

298

Greeting Cards

300

296...CREATE INEXPENSIVE ARTWORK BY DECOUPAGING GREETING CARDS ONTO STRETCHED AND PAINTED CANVAS SQUARES.

297.. CUT OUT GREETING CARD PICTURES AND PLACE IN ORNAMENTAL FRAMES.

298...DECOUPAGE GREETING CARDS TO TERRA-COTTA SAUCERS FOR GREAT COASTERS.

299

299...MAKE MAGNETS BY STIFFENING CUT-OUT GREETING CARDS AND ADDING BEADS, MINIATURE SPOONS, AND FLOWERS.

300...FRAME A FAVORITE GREETING CARD WITH AN OVERSIZED MAT FOR A LOOK STRAIGHT FROM AN ART GALLERY.

301...FILL A BASKET WITH CHERISHED CHRISTMAS CARDS AND PHOTOGRAPHS OF FAMILY AND FRIENDS.

301

302

302...DESIGN A BEAUTIFUL BOOKMARK WITH GREETING CARDS, RIBBON, AND LACE.

303...DECOUPAGE GREETING CARDS TO DRAWER FRONTS, THEN ATTACH PULLS.

304...GLUE A FAVORITE GREETING CARD TO BOTTLE FRONT FILLED WITH MATCHING CONTENTS AND GIVE AS A HOSTESS GIFT.

305...CREATE A COLORFUL MOSAIC, USING TINY GREETING CARD PIECES DECOUPAGED TO THE INSIDE OF A VASE.

304

303

305

306

307

308

Flowers

306...FILL A LARGE BASKET WITH LAVENDER
TO DECORATE AN OUTDOOR GATHERING AS
WELL AS BRING A DELIGHTFUL SCENT.

307...DRIED PURPLE PANSIES MAKE A DELICATE
LAMP SHADE FOR SPRING.

308...USE ASPARAGUS OR OTHER VEGETABLES
TO DECORATE WITH IN PLACE OF FLOWERS.

310

309

309...SCENT GUEST
TOWELS WITH DRIED
ROSES TIED IN
MATCHING RIBBONS.

310...DISPLAY FLOW-
ERS IN DISCARDED
SODA BOTTLES.

311

311...USE YOUR DRIED WEDDING FLOWERS TO HELP PRESERVE THE MEMORIES OF YOUR WEDDING DAY.

312...MAKE MINIATURE DRIED FLORAL WREATHS TO ADORN BOTTLES FILLED WITH OILS AND FLAVORED SUGARS.

313...FOR A SPECIAL OCCASION, MAKE A LIVING ROSE WREATH.

313

312

314

314...ENHANCE A CURTAIN AND ADD FRAGRANCE TO A ROOM BY USING FLOWERS AS CURTAIN TIEBACKS.

315...PLACE DRIED FLOWERS BETWEEN TWO PIECES OF GLASS IN AN OLD PICTURE FRAME, SECURE, AND USE AS A SUMMER SERVING TRAY.

315

316

317

318

Candy

320

319

316...USE A CHILD'S NEW TRUCK TO SERVE YOUR FAVORITE BONBONS.

317...DECORATE WITH A CANDY CANE TREE.

318...WRAP A GIFT WITH A CANDY CANE BOW OR LICORICE TIE.

319...FILL A JAR WITH CANDY FOR A FUN DRESSER ADDITION.

320...DECORATE A TREE WITH CANDY CANE ORNAMENTS.

Candy

80

321

321...DAZZLE CHILDREN WITH A CANDY TRAIN.

322...BRING SURPRISE TO A TABLE SETTING BY ADDING A LOLLIPOP TO THE SILVERWARE.

322

323

323...THRILL VISITING CHILDREN WITH CANDY AIRPLANES.

324...SWEETEN A FAVORITE PICTURE OR CARD WITH A FRAME OF CANDY STICKS.

325...ADD A FUN TOUCH TO COLORFUL PARTY PARFAITS WITH LOLLIPOPS.

324

325

Candy

326

Birdhouses

327

327

329

330

328

326...ADD INTEREST TO A BIRD-HOUSE WITH SHELLS.

327...CREATE A CHARMING CHEST-OF-DRAWERS BIRDHOUSE AS MIKE DILLON DID ON THIS MANTELPIECE.

328...MAKE A DELIGHTFUL POTTING BENCH WITH BIRD-HOUSE LEGS.

329...BRING CHARACTER TO A RUSTIC BIRDHOUSE WITH A LICENSE PLATE ROOF.

330...BRING COLOR INTO ANY ROOM BY HANGING AN ORIENTAL BIRD CAGE.

331...USE TRIPLE-DECKER BIRDHOUSES TO MAKE STURDY, FUN TABLE LEGS.

332...A WOODEN BIRD-HOUSE MADE WITH VARIOUS ANTLERS MAKES FOR BEAU-TIFUL GARDEN ART.

333...ATTACH A CANDE-LABRA TO THE TOP OF A WHITEWASHED BIRD-HOUSE FOR AN INTEREST-ING CANDLELIGHT DINNER CENTERPIECE.

334...CREATE A FUNKY CERAMIC BIRDHOUSE AS MIKE DILLON DID HERE FOR THE GARDEN.

335...FOR HALLOWEEN, PLACE A CROW AND A MONSTER ON A BIRD-HOUSE TO WELCOME GUESTS.

Birdhouses

Marbles

336

336...DRESS UP AN OLD PICTURE FRAME BY ADDING MARBLES TO THE BORDER.

337...FILL THE BOTTOM OF A VASE WITH MARBLES TO ADD COLOR AND ACT AS A "FROG" FOR THE FLOWERS.

338...ADD COLOR TO A FOUNTAIN BY LETTING THE LIGHT ILLUMINATE MARBLES.

339...PLACE HORS D'OEUVRE FORKS AND SPOONS IN A GLASS FILLED WITH MARBLES.

340...COVER THE BOTTOM OF A CONTAINER WITH CLEAR MARBLES, THEN FLOAT A CANDLE ON THE WATER.

337

338

339

340

341...ADORN A METAL LAMP WITH COLORFUL MARBLES.

342...USE CLEAR MARBLES IN AN AQUARIUM.

343...FILL A CONTAINER WITH MARBLES TO STEADY A VOTIVE CANDLE.

344...TOP SMALL, DECORATIVE BOTTLES WITH CLEAR MARBLES.

345...DECORATE A VASE RIM WITH BRIGHTLY COLORED MARBLES.

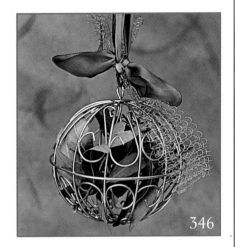

346

Ornaments

347

349

349...EMBELLISH A GIFT OR PACKAGE WITH GLASS ORNAMENTS.

350...SEW SMALL ORNAMENTS AND BOWS TO THE BOTTOM OF A VALANCE FOR A FESTIVE TOUCH.

350

346...FILL A WIRE ORNAMENT WITH POTPOURRI AND HANG IN THE BATHROOM OR CLOSET.

347...SURROUND A CANDLE IN A BASKET WITH COLOR-COORDINATING ORNAMENTS.

348...TIE ORNAMENTS RANDOMLY TO A RIBBON AND DRAPE AROUND WINDOW AS A GARLAND.

348

351...PERSONALIZE CHRISTMAS
TREE LIGHTS FOR EASTER DINNER
"PLACE CARDS."

352...USE CHRISTMAS ORNAMENTS
TO DECORATE FOR ANNIVERSARIES.

353...USE AN ORNAMENT AS A TOPPER FOR A DECORA-
TIVE JAR.

354...TIE ORNAMENTS TO NAPKINS FOR NAPKIN RINGS.

355...FILL A GLASS CONTAINER WITH BEADED FRUIT
ORNAMENTS AND PLACE ON TOP OF A GARDEN
PEDESTAL FOR A SPIRITED CENTERPIECE.

356

357

358

Shells

360

359

356... DRILL TINY HOLES IN LARGER SHELLS AND STRING TOGETHER WITH RIBBON TO HANG ON CHAIR BACKS.

357...ADORN A FRAME BY GLUING TINY SHELLS ON FRAME FRONT.

358...STRING SHELLS LIKE A NECKLACE TO MAKE A BEAUTIFUL CURTAIN TIEBACK FOR THE SUMMER MONTHS.

359...FILL A GLASS VASE WITH LARGE SHELLS TO ACT AS A "FROG" IN A FLOWER BOUQUET.

360...PAINT SEASHELLS TO RESEMBLE EASTER EGGS AND DISPLAY FOR THE HOLIDAY.

361...USE A VARIETY OF SHELLS AS DRAWERS PULLS.

361

362...GLUE CLAMSHELLS TOGETHER AROUND EACH LIGHT ON A CHRISTMAS LIGHT STRAND TO MAKE SUMMER PATIO LIGHTS.

363...USE SHELLS AS A GARDEN BORDER.

364...DECORATE THE BOTTOM OF A VASE FULL OF DELICATE FLOWERS.

365...ADHERE SHELLS TO A FAUX-PLASTERED WALL TO ACT AS A CHAIR RAIL FOR AN ADDED DETAIL TO WALL DÉCOR.

Sports

367

366

368

366...OLD GYM LOCKERS MAKE A CLOSET OR STORAGE UNIT THAT A YOUNG SON MIGHT EVEN USE!

367...USE AUTHENTIC MAJOR LEAGUE BASEBALL BATS AS THE BALUSTERS OF A RAILING IN A SPORTS ROOM.

368...STORE EXTRA BILLIARD BALLS IN MOUNTED SNOWSHOES IN THE POOL ROOM.

369...RETIRE A MUCH-LOVED GOLF BAG TO THE FAMILY-ROOM WALL AS A CONTAINER FOR DRIED OR SILK FLOWERS.

370...THEATER SEATS MAKE THE PERFECT PLACE FOR THE AUDIENCE TO BE SEATED WHILE THE OPPONENTS SQUARE OFF FOR A CHAMPIONSHIP GAME OF PING-PONG.

371...USE VINTAGE SKI POLES AS CURTAIN RODS, SNOWSHOES TO ADD ACCENT, AND VINTAGE SKIS FOR INTEREST.

372...DRESS UP A BASEBALL-LOVER'S BED-SPREAD WITH BASE-BALLS STITCHED TO SMALL THROW PILLOWS.

373...SPELL OUT A CHILD'S NAME ON THE BEDROOM WALL WITH INEXPENSIVE GOLF CLUBS.

374...WELD HORSE-SHOES TOGETHER TO MAKE A RUSTIC COAT HANGER.

375...USE OUTGROWN SPORT UNIFORM SHIRTS AS FUN GEAR BAGS FOR NEW SPORTS.

376...DISPLAY SPORTS EQUIP-
MENT AS PART OF A ROOM'S
DÉCOR.

377...TURN A SMALL FISHING
BASKET INTO A MUSICAL BOX.

378...OUTGROWN SKIS MAKE
A FUN HEADBOARD AND
HANGER FOR ANY SPORTS
ENTHUSIAST.

379...TRANSFORM AN OLD
FISHING POLE AND REEL INTO
AN INTERESTING WIND CHIME.

380...ADHERE FAVORITE
POSTERS TO WINDOW BLINDS.
WHEN KIDS ARE AT SCHOOL
THE BLINDS CAN BE OPENED
AND THE SUN CAN SHINE
THROUGH UNOBSTRUCTED.

Hardware

381...SUSPEND PIECES OF REBAR FOR AN UNUSUAL AND STURDY CURTAIN ROD.

382...DISPLAY YOUR COLLECTIONS, EVEN IF THEY ARE SOMEWHAT "UNTRADITIONAL", SUCH AS AN ANTIQUE SAW.

383...MOUNT A SECTION OF CHAIN-LINK FENCE FOR A UNIQUE HEADBOARD.

384...WELD A COLLECTION OF METAL PARTS TOGETHER TO MAKE AN EYE-CATCHING LAWN ORNAMENT.

385...TURN A WATER FAUCET AND WATERING CAN INTO A SMALL FOUNTAIN FOR INSIDE OR OUT.

386...THREAD BED SHEETS THROUGH PLATE HOLDERS FOR AN INEXPENSIVE WINDOW TREATMENT.

387...ASSEMBLE A COLLECTION OF DOOR HARDWARE FOR A UNIQUE TOWEL AND ROBE RACK.

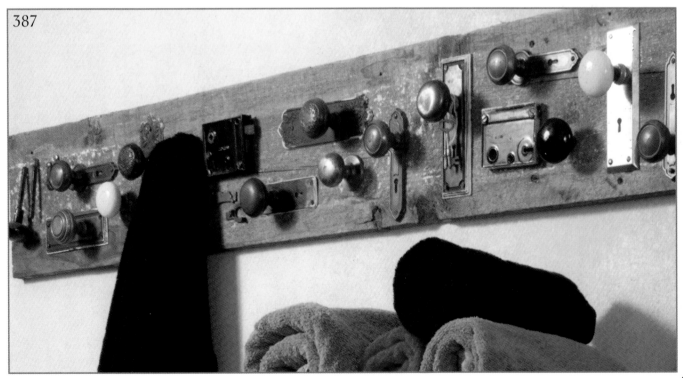

388

388...ACCENTUATE A WESTERN
WINDOW TREATMENT WITH
ANTIQUE DOORKNOBS.

389...STACK YOUR FLOWERPOTS
ON AN ANTIQUE WOODEN LADDER,
OR A PAINTED NEW ONE, TO BRING
THE "OUTSIDE IN."

390...TURN A LIGHT SOCKET INTO
AN INTERESTING CANDLESTICK.

389

390

Crates

391...MAKE SETTING THE
TABLE EASY BY KEEPING
NAPKINS AND SILVERWARE
IN A HANDY PAINTED CRATE.

392...MOUNT A PAINTED
OLD VEGETABLE CRATE ON
THE WALL TO ACT AS A
SHELF FOR POTTED PLANTS.

393... FASHION A CRATE
WITH A LID AND USE THE
BOX TO HIDE THE GARDEN
HOSE WHEN NOT IN USE.

394...USE AN OLD CARPENTER CRATE AS "GIFT-WRAPPING" FOR THE TOOL LOVER.

395...TRANSFORM AN OLD CRATE INTO A COMFORTABLE FOOT STOOL.

396...USE A TOOL CRATE TO HOLD POTS AND PLANTING SUPPLIES TO CARRY AROUND THE YARD.

397...ADD A SPECIAL TOUCH TO KITCHEN CANDLES BY PLACING THEM IN TERRA-COTTA POTS IN A VINTAGE FLOWER CRATE.

398...PLANT SUMMER ANNUALS IN A RUSTIC OLD CRATE—THE CONTRADICTION IN A NICE ONE.

399...IF YOU ARE A PAINTER, PAINT A HANDLED CRATE AND USE TO HOLD ALL OF YOUR PAINTING SUPPLIES.

400...STORE A CHILD'S "TREASURES" IN A HANDMADE CRATE WITH CHICKEN WIRE SIDES AND PAINTED THE CHILD'S FAVORITE COLOR.

Chairs

401...KEEP STRAIGHT PINS CLOSE BY WITH A SMALL, CUSHIONED ROCKING CHAIR.

402...GIVE HEIGHT AND EXPOSURE TO A COLLECTIBLE BY STACKING IT ON A MINIATURE CHAIR.

403...CREATE A BEAUTIFUL CHAIR PLANTER BY WRAPPING IT WITH TORN STRIPS OF FABRIC. CUT A HOLE IN THE WOODEN SEAT AND COVER WITH FABRIC. PLACE A PAINTED POT THROUGH THE HOLE.

404...MOUNT AN INVERTED CHAIR TO THE WALL FOR DISPLAYING SPRING FLOWERS.

405...USE A PAINTED DECORATIVE CHAIR IN THE BEDROOM AS A SMALL VANITY. MAKE A STOOL TO MATCH AND PLACE PAINTED POTS WITH COTTON SWABS ON THE CHAIR FOR EASY ACCESS.

406...DISPLAY MEMENTOS ON AN UNUSED, ANTIQUE CHAIR.

407...USE A HAND-PAINTED CHAIR IN THE BATHROOM TO KEEP CLEAN BATH TOWELS EASILY ACCESSIBLE AND TIDY.

408...SECURE A GROUPING OF SMALL CHAIRS ON THE WALL, THEN DISPLAY SMALL TREASURES.

409...GROUP VOTIVE CANDLES TOGETHER WITH MINIATURE CHAIRS.

406

407

408

409

410

410...PAINT POTS TO MATCH A DESIGNER CHAIR, THEN PLACE ON A COVERED PATIO TO ENJOY THROUGH THE SUMMER MONTHS.

Chairs

101

411

412

Photographs

413

411...WRAP FAMILY GIFTS IN PAPER PHOTO-COPIED WITH FAMILY PHOTOGRAPHS.

412...DECOUPAGE PHOTOCOPIED FAMILY PHOTOGRAPHS ON STORAGE BOXES CON-TAINING CHERISHED FAMILY PAPERS.

413...WRAP PHOTO-COPIED PHOTOGRAPHS AROUND NAPKINS AND TIE WITH RIBBON FOR UNUSUAL PLACE CARDS.

414

415

414...ROLL BLACK-AND-WHITE PHOTOGRAPHS INSIDE GLASSES AND DISPLAY IN KITCHEN HUTCH.

415...DECOUPAGE A BEACH PHOTOGRAPH TO THE CENTER OF A SOAP DISH.

416...EMBELLISH A SCREEN
WITH FAVORITE PHOTOGRAPHS.

417...MOUNT SPORTING PHO-
TOGRAPHS TO COAT RACK
HOLDING SPORTING GEAR.

418...BRING A CHERISHED PHOTOGRAPH TO THE
WORKPLACE BY TRANSFERRING IT TO THE MOUSE PAD.

419...USE A FAMILY PHOTOGRAPH AS THE LABEL FOR
GIFT OF A FAVORITE FAMILY RECIPE AND INGREDIENTS.

420...TRANSFER PHOTOGRAPH ONTO SQUARE OF
WHITE FABRIC, COVER WITH A LAYER OF ORGANDY,
TRIM WITH RIBBON, AND APPLIQUÉ TO PILLOW FRONT.

Frames

421...REPLACE DECORATIVE PIL-LOWS ON A BEDSPREAD WITH FRAMED PICTURES.

422...FRAME CORKBOARD IN A VINTAGE FRAME, THEN TACK STRIPS OF RIBBON TO SECURE NOTES, MESSAGES, AND MEMENTOS.

423...HANG "UNPICTURED" FRAMES AND VINTAGE NECKLACES FOR AN ECLECTIC WALL DISPLAY.

424...SECURE AN EMPTY FRAME ABOVE A DRAPED BED FOR ADDI-TIONAL INTEREST.

425

426

427

428

429

425...PAINT A GROUP OF EMPTY FRAMES THE SAME COLOR CREATING THE LOOK OF EXPENSIVE MOLDING.

426...FRAME FABRIC IN HEAVY FRAMES, COVER BACK WITH FELT, AND USE AS PLACE MATS.

427...USE A CHERISHED FRAMED PHOTOGRAPH AS A UNIQUE PLACE CARD.

428...FILL A STAIRWAY WALL FROM LANDING TO CEILING WITH MATCHING FRAMES AND PHOTOGRAPHS.

429...ENHANCE THE GARDEN WITH A FRAMED BIRDHOUSE.

430...TURN A WOODEN-FRAMED PICTURE INTO A JEWELRY BOX LID.

430

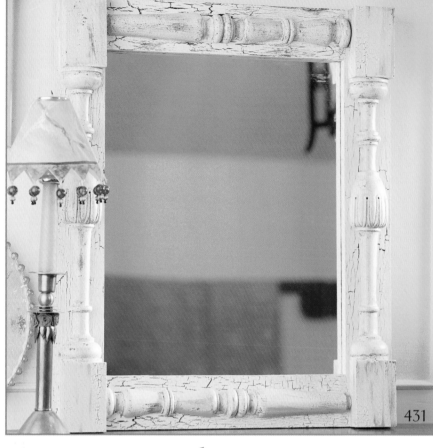
431

431...CUT BALUSTERS IN HALF, GLUE TO WOODEN FRAME, DISTRESS, AND BORDER A MIRROR.

432...COLLECT WEATHERED BALUSTERS, DRILL HOLES IN TOP END, AND FILL WITH CANDLECUP AND CANDLE FOR AN INDOOR OR OUTDOOR SET OF CANDLEHOLDERS.

433...CUT BALUSTERS IN HALF TO ADD DECORATIVE BORDERS TO A BAR OR BUTCHER BLOCK.

434...SUPPORT DEN SHELVES WITH BALUSTERS IN ASSORTED SIZES.

Balusters
& Finials

432

433

434

435

437

437...BRIGHTLY COLORED FINIALS MAKE GREAT DECORATING ACCESSORIES.

438...DESIGN A GARDEN FENCE USING BALUSTERS AND HEADBOARDS.

438

435...USE A FANCY BALUSTER IN THE MIDDLE OF A RAILING TO ADD INTEREST.

436...ADD A CHARMING TOUCH TO A PLANTER BOX WITH FINIAL ENDS.

436

439...CONNECT SEVERAL BALUSTERS AND SUSPEND AS A CURTAIN ROD TO DRAPE GAUZE OVER AS ACCENTS FOR WOODEN SHUTTERS.

440...ADD A TOUCH OF DESIGN TO AN OLD TOOL BOX WITH A BALUSTER HANDLE.

Light Fixtures

441

442

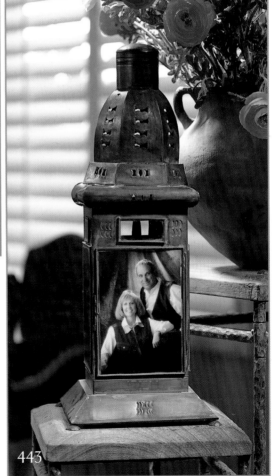

443

441...HANG A VINTAGE CRYSTAL CHAN-
DELIER ON A PATIO FOR ELEGANT OUT-
DOOR LIGHTING DURING THE HOLIDAYS.

442...AN INVERTED, BEADED LAMP
SHADE PLACED ON A CANDLESTICK GIVES
OFF A BEAUTIFUL GLOW WHILE THE CAN-
DLE BURNS.

443...PLACE A FAMILY PHOTOGRAPH
INSIDE AN UNUSED LANTERN AS A
DESIGNER "FRAME."

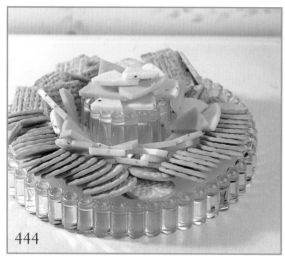

444...CONVERT A GLASS LIGHT COVER INTO A STYLISH CHEESE AND CRACKER SERVING TRAY.

445...OLD FLOOR LAMPS WITH POTS IN PLACE OF ATTACHED TABLES AND LAMP SHADES MAKE OUTDOOR PLANTERS THE ENTIRE NEIGHBORHOOD WILL LOVE.

446...A VINTAGE GLASS LAMP MAKES A CHARMING BIRDSEED HOLDER TO HANG FROM THE PORCH.

447...GLASS LAMP COVERS ARE HUNG UPSIDE DOWN WITH BEADED CHAINS TO BECOME RETRO HANGING CANDLE-HOLDERS.

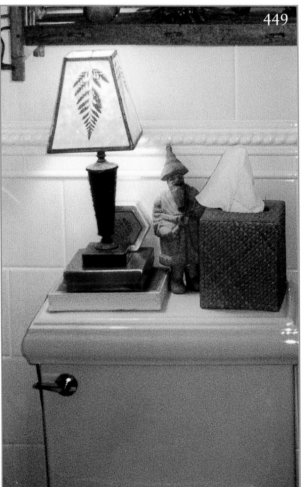
449

448...SECURE GLASS LIGHT COVERS TO A WALL WITH GLASS BUTTONS FOR A SHABBY-CHIC DECORATOR'S TOUCH.

449...BRING A SMALL DESK LAMP INTO THE BATHROOM FOR A SOFT NIGHTLIGHT.

450...MAKE WONDERFULLY ELEGANT CAN-DLEHOLDERS WITH OLD METAL LAMPS.

450

Light Fixtures

Iron Gates & Fences

451

452

451...HEART HEADBOARD MAKES A
UNIQUE FENCE OR GATE.

452...MAKE A STYLISH FIREPLACE SCREEN
WITH A PORTION OF AN OLD GATE.

454

455

453...USE AN ORNATE IRON GATE IN A WINDOW IN PLACE OF CURTAINS.

454...DECORATE ANY ROOM, EVEN THE BATHROOM, WITH AN OLD IRON GRATE.

455...AN IRON GATE MAKES A GREAT BACKYARD TRELLIS.

Iron Gates & Fences

Furniture

456...ATTACH A COF-
FEE TABLE TO THE
KITCHEN CEILING TO
USE AS A DESIGNER
POT RACK.

457...USE A RICH-
GRAINED DOOR,
SECURED TO THE WALL,
TO ACCENTUATE A
GROUPING OF FRAMED
PICTURES.

458...STACK SEVERAL
OUTDOOR BENCHES IN
FRONT OF A WINDOW
AND USE AS "SHELVES"
TO DISPLAY MEMENTOS
AND COLLECTIBLES.

459...PLACE A HEADBOARD
BETWEEN THE LIVING ROOM AND
AN OUTDOOR PATIO WHEN MORE
PRIVACY IS REQUIRED.

460...MOUNT A PENCIL
DRAWER TO THE WALL. DRILL
AND SECURE DOWELS TO DIS-
PLAY A COLLECTION OF
DIPPED CANDLES.

461...AN ANTIQUE BUREAU
IN A KITCHEN ALCOVE BRINGS
DESIGN AND FUNCTION.

462...TAKE AN UNUSED END
TABLE INTO THE BATHROOM
FOR STORING EXTRA TOWELS
BY THE BATHTUB.

Furniture

115

463

464

463...A WOODEN HEAD-
BOARD USED AS A BACKDROP
TO A BUREAU TOP BRINGS A
RICH LOOK INTO THE ROOM.

464...RESTAIN AND MOUNT
OLD CUPBOARD DOORS ON A
HALLWAY WALL TO RESEM-
BLE EXPENSIVE MOLDING.

465..."PLANT" A BRASS BED
IN THE GARDEN FOR A
PERENNIAL BED OF FLOWERS.

465

Furniture

466

Windows

466...USE A WINDOW AS A HOLIDAY DÉCOR BACKDROP.

467...ARRANGE DRIED FLOWERS AROUND AN OLD WINDOW FRAME TO REPLACE A TRADITIONAL PICTURE.

468...PLACE A WINDOW BEHIND FRAMED ART FOR ADDED INTEREST.

467

468

469

469...HANG A FRAMED PICTURE ON TOP OF AN OLD WINDOW TO ADD SOMETHING NEW TO YOUR DECO-RATING SCHEME.

470

471

472

470...TAPE PHOTOGRAPHS TO THE GLASS PANES OF OLD WINDOW.

471...HANG SALVAGED STAINED-GLASS WINDOWS FROM A BEAM INDOORS OR OUT.

472...ADD PRESSED LEAVES AND A PHOTO TO EACH OF THE PANES OF AN OLD WINDOW.

473...USE A WINDOW THAT RECEIVES A LOT OF SUN AS A SHOWPLACE FOR CHERISHED DISHES AND COLLECTIBLES.

473

474

475

474...CREATE A SOLARIUM FOR PLANT STARTS BY PLACING A WINDOW OVER A WOODEN BOX.

475...DISPLAY PHOTOGRAPHS OR PICTURES IN WINDOWPANES AND MOUNT INSIDE OR OUT.

476

477

Doors, Screens

& Shutters

MUSTARD & OAT SCREEN

478

476...A ROLLED SCREEN MAKES A BEAUTIFUL BASKET TO HOLD BERRIES AND LEAVES.

477...HANG AN OLD SCREEN DOOR TO DISPLAY TREASURED ANTIQUES.

478...PIN RIBBONS ACROSS A SCREEN DOOR TO HOLD PHOTOGRAPHS IN PLACE FOR A FUN DISPLAY.

479...MAKE A POTPOURRI HOLDER BY CUTTING A HEART SHAPE FROM AN OLD SCREEN AND ADORN WITH BEADS, FLOWERS, AND BUTTONS.

479

480...HINGE TWO OR MORE DOORS TOGETHER AND USE AS A "SCREEN" TO BLOCK THE VIEW INTO ANOTHER ROOM.

481...PAINT A SCREEN DOOR TO ADD TO THE GARDEN.

480

481

WELCOME

482

482...CONVERT AN OLD WEATHERED DOOR INTO A DINING-ROOM TABLE.

483...A SINGLE SHUTTER GIVES A GROWING IVY AN INDOOR CLIMBING POST.

484...PLACE FRESH FLOWERS, VEGETABLES, AND SPICES IN THE RUNGS OF A SHUTTER TO LET THE AIR CIRCULATE WHILE DRYING.

485...SHUTTERS ATTACHED TO A WALL MAKE A PERFECT OUT-OF-THE-WAY CD HOLDER.

486...PAINTED SHUTTERS, STRATEGICALLY PLACED, HIDE UNSIGHTLY WALL PROBLEMS.

487

487...HINGE SHUTTER DOORS TOGETHER AND PLACE IN CORNER TO HIDE POWER CORDS AND WALL SOCKETS.

488...KEEP SEED PACKETS CLOSE AT HAND BY PLACING SHUTTERS ON THE GARDEN WALL.

489...SERVING CHIPS AND DIP ON AN OLD SHUTTER "SERVING TRAY" HELPS KEEP CRUMBS OFF THE SERVING SURFACE.

490...WOODEN SHUTTERS MAKE A UNIQUE RAILING FOR BUNK BEDS.

488

489

490

Tiles

491

492

491...ONE OF A KIND COL-LECTIBLE TILES MAKE A BEAUTIFUL FIREPLACE.

492...DECOUPAGE A FAVORITE PICTURE ONTO A TILE WITH CHARACTER AND HANG.

493...USE A LARGE MARBLE TILE AS A CLASSIC SERVING TRAY.

493

494

495

496

494...MAKE A TREASURED IMPRINT OF A CHILD'S HAND ON TUMBLED STONE.

495...CENTER A FAMILY PHOTOGRAPH, ON A MARBLE TILE AND FRAME FOR AN UNUSUAL MEMENTO OF A BEAUTIFUL DAY.

496...SERVE DESSERT DIRECTLY ON A CLEAN TILE.

497...STACK SMALL TILES TO ADD DIMENSION IN A CURIO CABINET.

497

498

499

500

498...HAND-PAINT A DESIGN ON TILE OR TUMBLED STONE FOR COLORFUL COASTERS. APPLY FELT TO BACK TO PROTECT FURNITURE.

499...DESIGN A MOSAIC FROM TILE CHIPS.

500...USING MARBLE PIECES AND CANDLESTICK HOLDERS, ADD TWO SHELVES TO CREATE A PEDESTAL FOR DISPLAYING PLANTS.

Tiles

Index